WE'RE GONNA MAKE YOU WHOLE

Yasmine Van Wilt

WE'RE GONNA
MAKE YOU WHOLE

OBERON BOOKS
LONDON

First published in 2011 by Oberon Books Ltd

521 Caledonian Road, London N7 9RH

Tel: 020 7607 3637 / Fax: 020 7607 3629

e-mail: info@oberonbooks.com

www.oberonbooks.com

A catalogue record for this book is available from the British Library.

ISBN: 978-1-84943-131-6

Cover illustration and design by James Illman

Characters

ANTOINETTE: (Double cast with Chorus 3).
Mid-late twenties. Role originated by Yasmine Van Wilt

CHORUS 1: Mixed-race/Creole.
Early-mid twenties. Role originated by Jordan King.

CHORUS 2: White, Mid-late twenties.
Role originated by Kara Peters.

CHORUS 3: Mid-late twenties.

CURTIS: Mid-late twenties/early thirties.
Role originated by Lennard Sillevis.

EMCEE: (Double cast with Curtis).
Mid-late twenties/early thirties.

KELLY: (Triple cast with Chorus 2 and Nancy). Mid-late twenties.

NANCY: Mid-late twenties.

ROCHELLE: (Double cast with Chorus 1).
Mixed-race/Creole. Early-mid twenties.

Note:

.. Should be 2/3 of a complete beat.

… Is a full beat of silence in which the beat following emphasises rather than digresses from the preceding beat. In other words, there is not a change of thought indicated by this as there is in a *(Beat.)*

The use of the / indicates the overlap of lines.

'To' should be used as an emphasis whereas 'ta' should be used as a kind of contraction. They are in fact different words completely.

The same is true for 'my' and 'ma'.

We're Gonna Make You Whole was produced for the first time at the Acquire Arts in Battersea, London on 10th August 2011 with the following cast:

ANTOINETTE/CHORUS 3: Yasmine Van Wilt

ROCHELLE/CHORUS 1: Jordan King

NANCY/KELLY/CHORUS 2: Kara Peters

CURTIS/EMCEE: Lennard Sillevis

Director, Kara Peters

ACT I

SCENE 1

The three CHORUS LADIES face front, eyes down. They are dressed as divas – as a divine and not all together wordly trio. They wait for their introduction from the EMCEE. A picture of the State of Louisiana behind.

EMCEE: Welcome to Louisiana's very best kept secret, the House of Funk. Hailing from the deepest darkest corners of the Bayou Teche, raised on Cajun goodness and Creole soul – they've been through heaven and hell and back to be HERE – Delphine, Antoinette and Betty Sue – come on people, put your hands together for – 'The ORACLES' – take it home ladies.

The following is flirtatious…

CHORUS 1: *(Coy.)* This your first time in Louisiana?!

CHORUS 1: *(Sexily.)* Don't worry baby, we'll take real good care of you!

CHORUS 2: Down in our bayou country. You're gonna get yourself –

CHORUS 1: A nice little brain fog –

CHORUS 1: You'll forget about your wife and kids.

CHORUS 2: You'll forget about your whiny husband.

CHORUS 3: *(Sung.)* You'll just get LOST!

CHORUS 2: Maybe it's cause there's something eating your brain?

CHORUS 1: Or maybe it's because we'll treat you so good… you'll never wanna leave!

The lights rise on the CHORUS LADIES. CHORUS 1 plays the tambourine and triangle and CHORUS 2 begins dancing. CHORUS

3 hums the introduction to 'Swing Low.' As CHORUS 3 sings into the microphone, CHORUS 1 and CHORUS 2 dance behind, accompanying their movement with tambourines, castinets. They sing along on every 'Swing Low' and hum the Accompaniment all the way through. The dancing becomes more stylised, erotic with 'I Put A Spell On You' – CHORUS 1 AND 2 lean forward and hum their harmonies into their microphones.

CHORUS 1: Come on down, we'll have a big parade.

CHORUS 2: We're gonna go downtown.

CHORUS 3: *(Sung.)* AND ALL THAT JAZZ –

A beat. The CHORUS sing all together on each repetition of 'Oh Susannah'

CHORUS 3: *(Sung.)*

Oh Susannah,
don't you cry for me.
Bury me beneath
the old oak tree.
And cross these arms
that used to fight.
And bury me beneath
the old oak tree tonight.

Bullets light the sky
like shooting suns
and I stare into the night
well it's not my choice to fight
And I see him fall
barely a man at all.
And his young lead legs,
collapse dead weight.
He calls to a lover
he leaves behind
and curses, the man, that's me,
who's shot him blind.

Standing in the centre of the earth.
A lonely god sings a silent dirge.
But what of the hero slain?
Oh no, just one more young life taken.
Well, do I cry, do I feel remorse?
No, no. They say. This is the soldier's curse.

Oh Susannah,
don't you cry for me.
Bury me beneath
the old oak tree.
And cross these arms
that used to fight.
And bury me beneath
the old oak tree tonight.

A beat.

The CHORUS strip down for a moment, removing their hairpieces, etc...as they cross offstage.'

CHORUS 1: Can we get some whisky Tommy? We've got friends in…Hello you…

CHORUS 2: It'll only be that same old cheap-ass bourbon.

CHORUS 3: But you're welcome to have some.

CHORUS 1: It makes the story go down smoother.

CHORUS 2: We're glad you've come. We've been waiting for you…

CHORUS 3: Since the water turned black.

CHORUS 1: Guess we were hoping you'd come a little sooner.

The CHORUS laughs.

CHORUS 1: But no matter, you're here now.

CHORUS 2: And we know we can trust you to take the story back…

CHORUS 1: That's why you came right?

A beat.

CHORUS 1: Baby, we're about to get a little postmodern on you because we gotta whole LOT of perspective.

CHORUS 2: We been here…since – before people.

CHORUS 3: Since just after the Mississippi started to run her curves down to the salt – making the bayous…

A beat.

CHORUS 2: We can be anybody –

CHORUS 3: And nobody. But sugar – sometimes having a body is nice.

A beat.

CHORUS 2: So long's there's been a life force, there's been a Urizen – better known as THE Company.

CHORUS 3: Better known as THE Company.

CHORUS 1: THEY are the force who try to keep the natural world down –

CHORUS 3: And we are the natural world –

CHORUS 1: BUT WE will not be silenced.

A beat.

CHORUS 2: What THE Company have always told the people…

CHORUS 1: What they have always wanted you to believe…

CHORUS 2: Is that they know better than you. That there's nothing you can do to take them on –

CHORUS 3: That there's nothing you can do to take them on –

CHORUS 2: THE Company have always controlled the flow of information.

CHORUS 1: But they can't control us.

CHORUS 2: They're shit scared –

CHORUS 1: 'Cause we have the whole story...

CHORUS 3: And they know, eventually, the truth's gonna get free.

A beat.

CHORUS 2: When we were young, we could –

CHORUS 2: Throw out a line – let it zing through the air – and you'd fight out the biggest tuna, its scales shining in the sun like it was made of truth.

CHORUS 1: Catfish the size of dogs used to swim through our waters tickling us with their whiskers –

CHORUS 3: Dolphins. When we were children, we swam in Barrataria Bay with the pods – holding their dorsals as they sliced through the water...they were joy embodied...

CHORUS 2: There were pools – where thousands of shrimp, in their own crazy dance used to breed, on the bottom of the bayous – rising to the top as they grew. And you shoulda seen them in the noonday sun – they were silver on fire.

CHORUS 1: Mosquitoes the size of your face – we made them, to keep THE Company away!

They are examining the audience, searchingly.

A beat.

CHORUS 2: We were children when the people who would become the Cajuns came down the snaggle-toothed mouth of the Mississippi to hide from THE Company here in this land...

CHORUS 3: It wasn't the first time people came here hiding from THE Company. But back THEN...nobody from THE Company would follow.

CHORUS 1: The first people...helped them survive...what was then...our wild land.

CHORUS 1: Not everybody chose to come here.

CHORUS 1: Some arrived in chains.

CHORUS 1: And spent the centuries since they set foot on this soil fighting to be free.

CHORUS 1: Over time. We saw the people get a lotta the kinks out. This place came to be, on the whole...something beautiful.

CHORUS 3: Not perfect...we're not saying that –

CHORUS 2: *(Cheeky – and self-referential.)* But when the people lived from the land...the land gave them life..

CHORUS 2: And then, THE Company came here with their sugar lips – and they talked their way into this world.

CHORUS 2: Because they found something they wanted!

CHORUS 1: And we warned the people about THE Company...

CHORUS 3: Baby, we shouted until our lips bled –

CHORUS 2: And our lungs had no more give –

CHORUS 1: But no one listened.

CHORUS 2: So when...the Disaster came.

CHORUS 1: And the oil flowed –

CHORUS 2: And kept on flowing –

They all drink.

CHORUS 3: Everything went to all hell.

A beat.

The CHORUS read the tarot cards, drink and tell the future.

CHORUS 1: After the Disaster, the ones who lived on the Gulf. They knew from the start – what THE Company had done.

CHORUS 2: But THE Company – they told the people there was nothing to worry about.

CHORUS 3: And they bought out scientists.

CHORUS 2: And academics.

CHORUS 1: And Congressmen.

CHORUS 2: And teachers.

CHORUS 2: They told the people everything was fine.

CHORUS 1: And admirals.

CHORUS 2: And politicians.

CHORUS 3: And they told the people everything was fine.

CHORUS 1: And lawmakers.

CHORUS 3: 'Come on in, the water's fine.'

CHORUS 3: 150,000 barrels of oil –

CHORUS 1: Gushed out a day.

CHORUS 2: Every day for eight months.

CHORUS 1: That's enough to fill the Thames –

CHORUS 3: At high tide.

A very short beat.

CHORUS 2: But they TELL the people –

CHORUS 3: That everything IS fine.

CHORUS 1: What you've got to understand –

CHORUS 2: Is that THE Company?

CHORUS 1: They either buy you.

CHORUS 3: OR they kill you –

A beat.

CHORUS 2: For eight months, they sprayed the oil down, they sank it all under the water. Then, they sprayed the land and the people.

CHORUS 3: And now? They still spray –

CHORUS 1: After midnight, when they think –

CHORUS 2: The people won't notice?

CHORUS 2: The spray – it eats you alive. You could hear the
people –

CHORUS 1: And the pelicans –

CHORUS 2: And the manatees screaming –

CHORUS 2: When they spray –

CHORUS 1: If their throats hadn't been eaten through –

CHORUS 3: THE Company. They own the spray.

CHORUS 1: They tell the people…they have everything under
control. And they do –

CHORUS 2: They knew exactly what they were doing.

CHORUS 2: They KNOW exactly what they ARE doing.

CHORUS 3: Infanticide.

CHORUS 2: Fratricide.

CHORUS 1: Patricide.

   A beat.

CHORUS 3: Genocide.

CHORUS 1: The Gulf is a graveyard.

CHORUS 2: 'Come on in, the water's fine!'

   A beat.

CHORUS 1: THE Company has the people by the balls.

CHORUS 2: If you get in bed with the devil, you can count on
getting fucked.

   A beat.

CHORUS 2: With their shoulders to the ground, coughing
black. The people are walking petroleum, their blood is so
thick with it.

CHORUS 2: It's in the water.

CHORUS 1: And the crabs.

CHORUS 2: And the air.

CHORUS 2: It's in the babies who cough all night from pneumonia.

CHORUS 3: It's in the mothers who miscarry.

CHORUS 1: It's in the fathers whose ears bleed.

CHORUS 3: It's in the grandmothers with vertigo.

CHORUS 1: It's in the fishermen whose skin bleeds.

CHORUS 2: It's in the B&B keeper's bleeding bowels.

CHORUS 1: The Gulf is a graveyard...

CHORUS 3: But everything's okay right?

CHORUS 1: Tommy – baby, we're gonna need another bottle!

A beat. They drink more. TOMMY enters with more whisky.

CHORUS 2: Snappers with skin rot.

CHORUS 1: Beached whales.

CHORUS 2: Cypress shrivelled.

CHORUS 1: Starved sharks.

CHORUS 2: Floating dolphins.

CHORUS 1: Sea grasses sink.

CHORUS 3: Crabs choked.

CHORUS 2: The Gulf is a graveyard...

CHORUS 3: 'Come on in, the water's fine.'

A beat.

EMCEE: Please welcome back Delphine, Antoinette and Betty Sue –

They cross on as they begin creating the background melody with the tambourines, etc.

As the song begins, CHORUS 1 and CHORUS 2 begin an ecstatic dance to an earthy, funeral hymn.

CHORUS 3: *(Sung.)* Wade in the water.

Wade in the water now, children.

Wade in the water.

God's gonna trouble the water.

Well, who are these children all dressed in red?

God's a-gonna trouble the water

Must be the children that Moses led

God's a-gonna trouble the water.

Chorus

Who's that young girl dressed in white

Wade in the Water

Must be the Children of Israelites

God's gonna trouble the Water.

Chorus

Jordan's water is chilly and cold.

God's gonna trouble the water.

It chills the body, but not the soul.

God's gonna trouble the water.

Chorus

If you get there before I do.

God's gonna trouble the water.

Tell all of my friends I'm coming too.

God's gonna trouble the water.

As the song ends, the stage fades to blackout.

SCENE 2

The characters are unaware of each other.

CURTIS: I'm not sure…I understand what you want from
my testimony. *(Beat.)* I guess…I've been involved in this
problem from the start because. Well I was there for the
explosion. So…yes, I mean…It's affected me. *(Beat.)* I've
got brown spots all up and down my arms and legs. I went
to New York for my cousin's funeral. She was only – half

Cajun. And…for that whole week. I – I could breathe fine again…and the marks cleared.

ROCHELLE: I…I started taking samples pretty early on. It was…I just watched the water turn black. So – I asked around and I started working with some researchers at my school who were willing.

KELLY: My husband and I, we were pulling in maybe 30 or 40 thousand pounds of red snapper a year. And about the same amount of crab and oysters. We had…you know we had to rebuild everything after Katrina…so we'd finally got it all back – in those 5 years, and then bam – you know. For a while…we kept fishing because…we didn't know what else to do. We were pulling a lotta fish up – with skin rot. And…all sorts of problems because of the oil. So finally, I went to THE Company, and I told them I would not take no for an answer.

ANTOINETTE: I've got sores – all up and down my legs. And my arms and…I used to be – I was an actress…on that soap, *Days of Your Life*, – it wasn't ever gonna win me an Oscar or anything. But it was all I knew how to do…now, I mean. At first, they could cover up all the – it wasn't such a big deal…but then, when they started to spread. So they let me go. They fired all of the local cast. They film in California now.

SCENE 3

CHORUS 2 takes notes while CURTIS talks. She should have a very snooty, very harsh New York accent.

CHORUS 2: Do you have a history of mental illness in your family?

CURTIS: No –

CHORUS 2: You have said before that your mother was often prone to insomnia –

CURTIS: No. I said she did shift work at night –

A beat.

CURTIS: We were poor. She did. What she could. I don't think that counts as –

CHORUS 2: Lack of sleep can be a major trigger for all sorts of other/ psychological disturbances.

CURTIS: Disturbances?/

CHORUS 2: It can be caused by/...the abuse of legal and illegal substances.

CHORUS 2: When you were on the rig, did you ever drink to fall asleep?

CURTIS: No. I mean, everybody has a beer now and again, but –

CHORUS 2: Were you intoxicated the evening of the Disaster?

CURTIS: No –

CHORUS 2: Your co-workers have described your behaviour before the incident – as erratic, confused. They suggested you might have been using cocaine.

CURTIS: No – who said that? Was it THE Company guys? I always took my job seriously. I was a hard worker. I'd never slack on the job – ever. They're only saying that to –

CHORUS 2: We will need you to submit a urine sample.

CURTIS: A urine sample. NOW? Why? I already did one of them when they took me off the rig and that was clean? Why should I have to do another one now? –

CHORUS 2: You are experiencing psychological problems and we need to make sure that they are indeed resultant from what you experienced with THE Company – or if you are having problems which are unrelated to your former position as fireman. Afterall, you signed a waiver saying you were –

CURTIS: You are trying to paint me as a fucking NUTJOB who...fell asleep during his shift...and through his own negligence became party to THE DISASTER – I

didn't fall asleep on duty – I reported that there were…
inconsistencies – and THE Company. THOSE assholes
who pay your wage…they know very well that at least
twenty people before me – blew that little fucker of
a whistle…and what did they do? Umm…absolutely
nothing. That's why we have this problem. SO NO – I will
not take your piss test. And I will not be subjected to any
more of this ridiculousness –

A quick knock at the door. CHORUS 1 enters.

CHORUS 1: Is everything alright in here Dr. Melkin?

CURTIS: NO everything is not –

CHORUS 2: All moving according to plan, thank you Dr
Niccols.

CURTIS: According to what plan – hanh?

CHORUS 2: Here is your prescription for diazapanoline
ephinephrinolcholoride. You should take it in the morning
with a glass of water, but on an empty stomach. And don't
eat anything before you take the pill. Best to chew with
your mouth closed.

*She reaches towards him with the prescription. She crosses to CURTIS
and puts a pill in his mouth. He swallows. He becomes completely
and utterly 'out of it'. He hallucinates the following:*

*CURTIS falls forward, slumped. The CHORUS carry/drag him
offstage as they sing.*

CHORUS 3: *(Sung.)*
Buried in the ground.
Mother Earth will swallow you.
Lay your body down.

A blackout.

SCENE 4

ANTOINETTE: Is it rolling? *(Beat.)* I wake up sometimes and I just – want to run the hell away! But there is nowhere left on this damned planet that ain't been conquered! There isn't no patch of earth nowhere that some twat with a flag ain't put his name to. Even the Tristan de Cunha islands. You know, they got more penguins than people – and it's sixty degrees year round…My Dad he had a contract on the islands when he first started out…a tanker spilled and so they sent him to investigate the accident..there were all these dead oiled penguins, lying on their sides with their eyes wide. And their babies, they were still sitting next to their mothers…just crying out for them. That's a lot like some of the stuff I've seen around here. I've been helping my cousin collect samples. And they, THE Company, they go around and they cut the heads off all the dead wildlife because they can't be held liable for anything that doesn't have a complete spinal cord. But we still test them. There was this mother and baby dolphin. They were so bloated and purple, they were oozing crude outta their skin – it had literally busted their skin because it's so heavy – and they looked like monsters, all knotted and gnarled. We took 'em back to the labs and we done the tests…anyone can do them, they're so easy. You just gotta do a tissue sample. And – the shit they had in their bodies, it coulda killed 'em ten times over. We cried for hours after that…

SCENE 5

Dulac, Louisiana. ROCHELLE coughs, deeply. She is folding clothes and tidying. She has a stack of books lined next to her. She waits for CURTIS. She is preparing to break the news that she is pregnant. She takes out her pregnancy test and then puts it back in her pocket. She coughs again. This time it is so painful she has to stop folding. She rests for a moment, and finishing her washing, reads.

CURTIS – who is overwhelmed and can't process life – begins drinking as he enters.

A beat. ROCHELLE is distracted.

CURTIS: I can't stand this goddamned neighbourhood anymore. You can't drive down the street without seeing fifty 'For Sale' signs. The Parkers, the Fourchons, the Christies…they've all got their houses on the market. And Andy is trying to sell his Hog…and you know how he loves that damned machine. You remember what this place was like when we were in high school? It felt like…a person could could…accomplish something. Now, it doesn't feel like…anything's ever gonna be okay…

A beat.

CURTIS: And I talked to Jimmy Boudreaux and he only got $10 grand compensation from THE Company – total! *(Beat.)* They were saying they were gonna give us a whole year's wage, well that was a lotta bullshit. 'We're Gonna Make You Whole.' Where do they even come up with this shit?

A beat.

CURTIS: I'm gonna have to sell the truck.

ROCHELLE: If you've gotta sell it – then do it. We'll find a way.

CURTIS: I bet you will…just have to bat your eyes a little, hanh?

A beat. She is unnerved by his rudeness.

ROCHELLE: I made some dirty rice…if you're hungry.

A beat. He shotguns a beer and starts drinking another…

ROCHELLE: You been home two months baby. You gotta start thinkin' like you…

CURTIS: Like I'm one of you? –

A beat.

CURTIS: Well I ain't.

ROCHELLE: You ain't never gonna get –

He finishes another beer and starts to get pretty wasted.

CURTIS: I'm never gonna get what –

ROCHELLE: You've got to start thinking that life is here now… you have to look for a job at an inland department –

CURTIS: *(Raising his voice.)* Don't tell me what to do –

ROCHELLE: Enough Curtis –

CURTIS: You can't just snap your fingers…

She is upset and wants to get away from him. She is trying to get him to get up off of her books.

ROCHELLE: Will you get off of my books please?!

CURTIS: No I will not get off your books.

A long pause. He opens another beer and is gathering the courage to 'accuse her.'

ROCHELLE: I got the exams tomorrow, so will you let me have my books?!

CURTIS: Oh – you got a test tomorrow?

ROCHELLE: I've only got this one –

CURTIS: Is there something you might want to tell me, Rochelle?

A beat.

CURTIS: A man takes a dangerous job – working on the rig because he can earn twice as much. And it pains him to have to be off-shore to do two weeks on, two weeks off because he misses his wife. Well…his wife…she's living a good life. She wants to have her cake and eat it too. She says to herself she's gonna find another man, one who's maybe a little more suave. Maybe not so rough in the hands. *(Beat.)* Who is Jacob?

ROCHELLE: Jacob is my professor –

CURTIS: You must be getting real good grades hanh? Cause it looks he called you twice today…

ROCHELLE: He called to –

CURTIS: Now what/ sort of man –

ROCHELLE: /tell me –

CURTIS: I am willing/ to put up with a lot of things but –

ROCHELLE: Jacob called to tell me that I've been offered –
depending on my results…Kettering and Kettering – want
me.

Blackout.

SCENE 6

KELLY: I don't really know what you need for the testimony.
Do you – do you plan to make the records public? Okay.
Well. Ha…They say: 'We're gonna make you whole.' That
is straight-up bullshit. *(Beat.)* What have they offered?
(Beat.) Well…about thirty. *(Beat.)* We made a hundred
grand last year. We paid off the house. *(Beat.)* Of course we
can't crab anymore. *(Beat.)* NO – If I won't eat the crabs
or the oysters, how am I gonna feel good about myself if
I'm selling them to other people, knowing what's in 'em.
The crabs we pick up, they're black on the inside. You
crack the shells…and you can smell the oil. I wouldn't
want my nieces and nephews eating it. *(Beat.)* Hard to
believe people think all that oil just disappeared. *(Beat.)*
Shrimp – they're like the cockroaches of the sea. They're
delicious, but they are – bottom feeders. *(Beat.)* And they
just sponge in all those oils, and toxins – all the crap from
the dispersants *(Beat.)* You get the shrimp, out of the
water, you can see them lined, all the insides, they look
like they smoked thirty years. What people don't know
is that the THE Company are running a secret giant, free
abortion clinic. Right now, I'd actually like to have those
freaks – you know the ones that campaign at the offices –
that throw paint at the doctors – I'd like to have them on
my side. *(Beat.)* I…was three months. When I…lost the
baby. I was…still…I was nervous about…being a mother. I
wasn't sure I'd know what to do. I'm almost glad it's dead.
Because what kind of a world is this. I've had friends…
who also… And my sister. Her – she just had a little girl

Shelly. And she has birth defects. They don't know if…
(Beat.) She's so small, you can only touch her with one
finger through the incubator…She's – I almost don't know
what's worse. You get more attached when they're…they're
older and they…It's not a question a mother ever wants to
rationalise…

KELLY: I recently tried to get the attention of THE Company.
And…all anyone can ask me is, 'did I feel like I was
supported.' 'Do I think it made a difference?'

KELLY: Well, what do you think? I wouldn't have had to…
walk 1200 miles to get them to listen if they were open to
suggestion. *(Beat.)* I don't think…this is one person's fault.
This…is a whole system broke down.

KELLY: *(Beat.)* I get in my boat, down Barrataria Bay, and
I don't hear – egrets calling. I don't see the tails of fish
twitching on the horizon. I don't…there isn't much of
anything. Except the stink of oil, and – the burn, of your
eyes going dull because Corexit is eating your flesh. Most
people…they don't understand…

Blackout.

*The sounds of the underground, of the dark, of a kind of cave, of
being, quite literally six feet under.*

SCENE 7

*ROCHELLE lays centre stage. She coughs deeply, bringing up blood. She
lies on the ground very still, and then throws up into a bucket.*

ANTOINETTE crosses to ROCHELLE.

ANTOINETTE: Jesus baby! *(Beat.)* I'm sorry I took so long – I
only just got your message.

ROCHELLE coughs deeply again.

ANTOINETTE: Blows my mind why on earth you didn't tell me
sooner…

A beat. ANTOINETTE leans and sits behind ROCHELLE. She holds her as she wrenches and jerks with pain. ANTOINETTE pets and holds ROCHELLE.

ROCHELLE: I'm sorry – I –

A beat.

ANTOINETTE: Did you tell your Mom? I refuse to lie to her if she calls me. *(Beat.)* That woman has a built-in bullshit detector. *(Beat.)* I don't know if you've noticed, but lately she is straight up scary… *(Beat.)* My mother heard the message you left…on the house phone. Who calls a house phone these days, hanh? So…anyway, you can just about guess the whole family's gonna know in a minute. Maybe – it'd be better if they hear it from you…

ROCHELLE: No –

ANTOINETTE: What do you mean no? This is the only good news they've had all year –

ROCHELLE: It's not…everything is all wrong. *(Beat.)* Just don't tell anybody, alright?

She begins coughing deeply again.

ANTOINETTE: Come on. Come here…it's gonna be okay Chelle. It's gonna be fine. Don't worry now. I'm not going anywhere – okay. Just…breathe deep.

SCENE 8

NANCY hangs up the Cherri Foytlin and Tin Man paintings. She goes through her film footage. Her phone rings three times. She ignores it.

NANCY: *(The phone rings – but she answers it this time.)* Hello – who is this? Who –

She hangs up the phone.

NANCY: Why am I doing this? Why – am I doing this. Because somebody has to. Because if you stick your head in the sand, they win. They win. They say Nobodaddy…they say he's – I voted for him – I gave him my…They say

he's a puppet of THE COMPANY. Maybe he is. Maybe –
nothing will ever be as it seems, again.

Another beat.

*NANCY's film footage begins silently in the background. She edits
the interview.*

NANCY: My Mother was a swan…she's – now she has the lung
problem that everyone does. Her – ears, bleed when she
sleeps. She can't dance because…she has constant vertigo.
She was a principal in the New York City Ballet. She
broke her ankle in a car accident. And she came home…
back to Falls River, MA. Where she met my Father…
They retired early and got a place on the Gulf – right
on the water. She used to collect seashells – the smallest
most perfect cochinas you could imagine…she's made me
these necklaces from the shells. They can't. They put their
savings, all they had into that move. And now – they…
Dad's lost about twenty pounds. He had his ethol benzene
levels checked. *(Beat.)* The THE Company are refusing
anyone help who lives with the Gulf. They don't want us…
they don't want anyone to…I'm trying to raise the money
to bring them here. I – I don't know if you have ever
experienced. The people you care for most in the world – I
would gladly. Give my own life for them, to make them
safe. *(Beat.)* Nobodaddy – they…I've promised to sign
their papers. I just want my parents safe – -

A short pause.

NANCY: Some people say that only a…very talented artist can
do portraiture. That only someone who has been trained…
in the French style is capable of doing faces…in such detail.
But…I've never ascribed to that idea. I worked with the
people down here, from Grande Isle and Port Fourchon
and Lafayette, and – and they made these portraits – their
illustrations of what they've lost. *(Beat.)* I couldn't…sit
back and watch. I'm not from the Gulf *(She grows quiet and
nervous and turns within)*, but I grew up on the Atlantic, so
I know…If you're born on the water – she takes you over,
you become her. You'll never be happy, if you're far from

her. *(Beat.)* She whittles you down. You can't hide anything from the ocean. She'll batter you into her till she makes you her own. She'll round you out like a small stone, till you're swallowed whole...till there's just the shred of truth. *(Beat.)* Subjective as it is...I still think...in this case. There is one truth. And...I have watched and continue to watch them cover it up. There's nothing on the networks. They have elminated all signs of. I got this...I got persmission from THE COMPANY because they thought the paintings were going to support THE Company's message: 'Come on in...' When there are no words...when nothing can be said and no one will hear – at least...there will be this. I'm bringing the paintings to THE Company. I am going to show them – how not okay this is. If they – if they laugh at me. I will show them the pictures of the children. I will bring them the videos of the old women whose faces have been eaten by the spray. They spray at night...when they are sleeping. They are hoping they will die in their sleep.

The phone rings again. NANCY ignores it.

NANCY: I make documentaries...because I – we have to find a way...

A beat.

NANCY: To make the world understand. Surely, somebody cares – if people knew, they would care, right? They would do something?

NANCY goes over her video footage. We hear only the sound from the interviews.

The lights go low and then...and then the sound of heavy footsteps coming up the stairs. Blackout.

SCENE 9

ANTOINETTE: Yeah, they've threatened to burn my house down – to do...all sorts of things. Last week, one guy came up to me in WalMart in the hosiery section with a stocking on his head (while I was buying pantyhose – you

gotta appreciate the continuity, right?! So he says to me
that if 'I valued my life, I'be better shut up'. And then
he just disappeared down the $0.99 cent aisle. Ha...I've
heard all sorts of crazy crap...I used to be real afraid. But
not anymore. I used to stay up all night in my living room
holding my baseball bat – preparing for whoever might
come in my door...I'd have this nightmare that – some
big thug dressed in black would get outta one of them
Company cars you see everywhere these days...and that
he would come through my front door and shoot me in
the head. I didn't sleep for weeks...but now. I'm not scared
– of anything anymore. I feel like – there's nothing they
can do to stop this movement. Maybe – they can shut one
or two of us up...but they can't – they can't silence the
TRUTH – *(Beat.)* There's a comfort in that.

A beat.

ANTOINETTE: How close do you want to see the sores. *(Beat.)*
I guess you could say I've got a long-standing vendetta
against THE Company. I mean, they've pretty much
ruined my life. *(Beat.)* The day the plant blew up...I was
on my way to Texas City for Easter to see my parents.
They were contractors. So they were there – on loan to...
THE Company. I...Got in my car. Took the 45. Smelt the
salt, the air getting thick and hot. 'One More Time' playing
on the radio – Daddy loved Lynard Skynard. *(Beat.)* Got
my aunt in the car with me singin' along. Asphalt looked
like it was melting, heat coming off the highway. Like a
mirage. *(Beat.)* Swear I saw him there for a minute then
– rising off the ground, his skin – the same colour as the
clay either side...When I heard Daddy was dead. I knew
that was him saying goodbye. There wasn't nothing left of
Daddy. Momma was a wreck, so I had to...go and identify
him and all they had was a couple of teeth – that's how
they knew it was him, from his DNA. They erased every
trace of my Daddy's life, except for what still lives in the
people who loved him. *(Beat.)* We had a wake, and the
room was so full, there were people just standing outside.
(Beat.) But all I could think, when I was saying his eulogy

– was that – the explosion that killed him at the plant – it was 5,000 degrees. It melted him. There were more than 800 safety violations at the plant – that contributed to its explosion. *(Beat.)* I got a real good lawyer, in Texas City, Brandon Connors, and he helped me fight THE Company – I stood in front of the leaders of THE Company in a public hearing – and the result, was that THE Company was forced, legally, to increase their health and safety standards. So now, I can see – that even after losing Daddy. After all we did…nothing has changed. And this time, so many more lives will be lost.

Blackout.

SCENE 10

ROCHELLE has come home after a long day taking samples. She should be dressed in camouflage. She calls ANTOINETTE. She calls several times.

ROCHELLE: Antoinette – hello. If you're there. You really need to pick up baby.

A pause. ROCHELLE is ordering her things. Looking through her phone – sending messages like mad. CURTIS enters.

CURTIS: My wife, the duck hunter! What'd you catch?

A beat.

ROCHELLE: Did you hear that Darlene down at the bank, her sister died of septicaemia?

CURTIS: Jesus – are you serious?

ROCHELLE: Yeah, she and the baby…they found the levels of toxins in her were – she had like 5% petroleum in her blood. *(Beat.)* This makes 32 women I've counted so far… in Lafayette who have died because of it –

CURTIS: I'm sorry cher. *(Beat.)* Look – try not to take this the wrong way, but I…I'm wondering if it's doing you any good working on this –

ROCHELLE: It's what Kettering has hired me to – and apart from that, I straight-up refuse to just sit back –

ROCHELLE feels a bit dizzy. She reels. CURTIS catches her and sits her down.

CURTIS: You cannot keep running on empty Chelle...

He motions for her to come and lie back on him... She does, reluctantly.

CURTIS: Got that letter we've been waiting for. *(Beat.)* When they lift the moratorium...I'm gonna have to go back. But I'll...I and they think they have an inland job for me...I'd be...well, it would be probably in Lafayette.

A beat.

CURTIS: Did you hear me...baby? *(Beat.)* This is good news, right? I...thought you'd be pleased.

ROCHELLE: I am...I'm happy for you Curtis.

CURTIS: Is that it?..You're...what is going on? *(Beat.)* I thought we were maybe...you know –

He goes to kiss her. She freezes.

CURTIS: What's wrong?

ROCHELLE: I'm not...made of bricks you know. You can't just...treat me...like I'm –

CURTIS: You're...scared of me – ?

ROCHELLE: You ain't seen yourself when you come home all coked-up, out your head, saying – doing...

CURTIS: Jesus...I don't know how much more I can say than...I –

Beat.

CURTIS: I'm doing my best Rochelle. Please tell me that counts...for something –

ROCHELLE: Curtis, this isn't about –

CURTIS: Please. Come on baby. You just gotta – come here. See. This is me. This is the man who loves you – who...I do anything – to keep you happy and safe. We're gonna...I ain't nowhere's near perfect. Lord knows my faults got faults...but you gotta believe we're gonna get through this together – *(Beat.)* What's wrong. What's going on with you? Come on, it's me. Tell me...

ROCHELLE: I...can't get through to Antoinette.

CURTIS: Yeah...and...

A beat.

ROCHELLE: She's not answering her phone...I went by her place and the doors were all...unlocked. And, earlier I saw those – you know the cars she said she thought was – -well, I saw a couple of 'em driving down LaFontaine and I...

CURTIS: You cain't let your imagination run wild on you Rochelle.

ROCHELLE: It's just weird her not –

CURTIS: She probably just decided to evacuate outta the flood path.

ROCHELLE: You're talking about the woman who waited out Katrina on her roof – ?

CURTIS: The most simple answer's usually the right one.

ROCHELLE: Momma hasn't heard from her and neither has Aunt Claire –

CURTIS: Give her a few days. You know she don't...she got her own way of getting on with things.

ROCHELLE: Yeah, you're...you're probably right. *(Beat.)* I just have such a...I got this sorta sick feeling in my...

CURTIS: So your parents evacuating?

ROCHELLE: Yeah. Daddy's got the whole car...ready to go.

CURTIS: Probably a good idea.

ROCHELLE: Do you think we should?

CURTIS: Well, if we're definitely gonna get some flooding here. Then, course, but, if they just saying that we maybe get some run-off, then…well, I dunno that if it's worth going anywhere. We're pretty high up –

ROCHELLE: Yeah, but we don't wanna be trapped in here… without a way down. I mean, what if…

A beat.

ROCHELLE: Well, you know…with the electricity and all…

CURTIS: It's perfectly safe Chelle…

ROCHELLE: I don't know…when the water comes up – it's gonna raise all the spray up. I don't wanna be around if that's coming here –

CURTIS: It's not gonna come here –

ROCHELLE: And how do you know?

CURTIS: And where do you wanna go?

ROCHELLE: I dunno – Momma and Daddy are going to Texas.

CURTIS: Well…we ain't got the money.

ROCHELLE: We should go with my parents –

CURTIS: I refuse – I don't want to have to –

ROCHELLE: You refuse? Get off your freaking high horse Curtis –

CURTIS: I refuse to be indebted to your parents AGAIN –

ROCHELLE: Well, you couldn't ask your parents could you? –

CURTIS: You can't just run to them everytime we have a problem.

ROCHELLE: They're my parents, they WANT to help –

CURTIS: I'M YOUR HUSBAND –

ROCHELLE: This is bigger than –

CURTIS: Can you once, in our damned marriage discuss things with me – SOLVE problems with me, instead of being a little spoiled –

ROCHELLE: Fuck you!

She storms out of the house.

A beat. Fade to the next scene...

SCENE 11

On his porch alone, CURTIS plays. He chews tobacco, sunflower seeds and drinks whisky, does lines of coke and plays and cries...in no particular order.

CURTIS: *(Sung.) (CURTIS' song.)*

Blackout.

SCENE 12

CURTIS: You're back.

A beat.

CURTIS: I'm sorry.

She throws her bags down.

CURTIS: Am I getting the silent treatment now –

A beat.

CURTIS: I gotta go soon –

A beat.

CURTIS: I'm sorry baby. You're...right. We'll do whatever you think is right, okay?

A beat.

CURTIS: Alright?

ROCHELLE: Yeah...yeah.

He crosses to her and kisses her.

She kisses back, although, reluctantly.

CURTIS: I can't find all the documents. You file out that paperwork?

A pause. She is annoyed to have to jump into this conversation.

ROCHELLE: No, you're gonna have to look at it 'cause – they need like five years worth of documentation. I don't think we got it baby –

CURTIS: Well, that's great.

ROCHELLE: They're asking something about money we could have potentially earned – and we have to take that out of our claim?

CURTIS: What? Baby, can't you just figure it out? I got a whole pile of –

ROCHELLE: Well, I can't you only gave me about half of what I need to –

CURTIS: Well, I gave you all I got…

ROCHELLE: Curtis / – if you could just go through –

CURTIS: I gave you / what I got –

ROCHELLE: / Tax returns…your severance package. How much you pay out for your dependents. And then, you have to factor in the sale of the motorcyle, how much you're losing on the other property with it not being let. It's like 100 pages –

CURTIS: Jesus –

A beat.

ROCHELLE: You also…you gotta subtract what you got paid to do the clean-up.

CURTIS: I have to subtract what I got paid to clean-up THEIR mess from my compensation claim?

ROCHELLE: I called the help –

CURTIS: Are you telling me – that they are gonna take out the money they owe me because I worked to clean-up THEIR disaster?

A beat.

CURTIS: You have gotta be f – this is a fucking joke. *(Beat.)* SO I am literally – in the real use of the word – working off my own compensation money…and doing their dirty work at the same time?

A beat.

CURTIS: Well look at me.

A beat.

CURTIS: Your husband is the biggest mug that anybody ever saw. Not bad enough they try to goddamned blow me up? Not good enough is it…unbelievable.

ROCHELLE: Well, can you please call them up and say that – can you tell them…because I can't…

CURTIS: I don't have time / To call them? Because I have to go back out on that damned boat again. *(His nose starts bleeding. He blots it.)* And clean-up their toxic shit. SO can you...can you please – take a little f...reaking responsibility, please Chelle? And just do this for us?

ROCHELLE: This is not my fault –

CURTIS: Well what am / I supposed to do –

ROCHELLE: Stop cleaning up...for Godsake. / We don't need the money so badly that you should –

CURTIS: Yes, we do baby – we NEED the money that bad. We need it really effing bad baby. *(Beat.)*

ROCHELLE: Is anything worth putting youself in such a –

CURTIS: They are gonna find a way to take whatever / they can from me anyway –

ROCHELLE: Please – just stay / five minutes so we can –

CURTIS: I got...50 bags of oiled boom...which I can tell you is actually made from 1000 pairs of old tube socks in my truck – waiting to get taken down to the landfill. / So unless you want to let that melt into our driveway –

ROCHELLE: Curtis –

She drops to her knees and begins experiencing deep, painful pangs in her uterus. She shakes involuntarily as the pain grows. She lets out a deep gutteral cry. CURTIS holds her. He attempts to pick her up. A pool of blood begins gathering beneath her...

Blackout.

SCENE 13

The chorus fix their hair and makeup.

A beat.

CHORUS 2: Didn't think we'd forgotten about you, did ya – ?

CHORUS 1: We are – delighted to come back on and do another song for ya'll…

CHORUS 1: You know my sister Betty Sue –

CHORUS 2: You know my sister Delphine –

CHORUS 3: Well, they got something real special prepared for you tonight. Trained in the bayou school – in the primordial style…

CHORUS 1 and CHORUS 2 begin dancing and getting into the tune as CHORUS 3 starts humming:

CHORUS 3: There's no riches,
and there's no glory.
No happy ending to my story.
A tale of sadness and a tale of woe.
I lost my true love in the Gulf of Mexico.///

I'm a small town girl.
From Isle Jean Charles.
Married my sweetheart Pierre.
Jus' pre de Bayou Teche.///
They called at midnight.
To tell me that/
my one true love
is never coming back.///
There's no riches, and there's no glory.
No happy ending to my story.
A tale of sadness
and a tale of woe.
I lost my true love
to the Gulf of Mexico.

At night I dream
he calls my name.
A burning pyre,
engulfed in flames.
There's no riches,
and there's no glory.
No happy ending
to my story.
A tale of sadness
and a tale of woe.
I lost my true love
to the Gulf of Mexico.

CHORUS 2: Ya'll be sure to stay for the shrimp broil after.

CHORUS 1: Be a dinner to remember –

They all find this hysterical. They begin to cross off. CHORUS 1 and CHORUS 2 dance and warm-up, getting ready to go on.

They pass their bottle of bourbon between them and take a great long swig.

CHORUS 1: Ya'll don't go nowhere. We're just gonna freshen up…

Blackout.

The CHORUS disappear below. The next scene takes place downstairs.

Curtain.

ACT II

SCENE 1

Standing ahead of the audience is Nancy. She edits her footage from interview one.

Blackout. She exits back into her cave.

SCENE 2

CHORUS 2 and CHORUS 3 sit next to two telephones. They make the sounds of the phone ringing and then answer – -Their voices answering the phones should create a kind of chorus. They should speak over each other constantly.

CHORUS 2: Office of THE Company. This is Candy. / How may I direct your call?

CHORUS 3: Good afternoon, Nobodaddy's office. This is Wilma. How may I assist you?

CHORUS 2: Yes, / hold please.

CHORUS 3: Hold please.

CHORUS 3: I'm afraid/

CHORUS 2: Nobodaddy is out –

CHORUS 3: You can leave a message if you'd like.

CURTIS and ROCHELLE enter. The phones ring again.

CHORUS 2: Hold please.

CHORUS 3: Nobodaddy is out.

CURTIS: *(Crossing Forward.)* Now look here –

CHORUS 2: *(Speaking into the phone and to CURTIS at the same time.)* Nobodaddy is out to lunch.

CHORUS 2: If you would like to leave a message I'll be sure –

CHORUS 3: He's a very busy –

ROCHELLE: I want to speak to your manager NOW –

CHORUS 2: For what –

CHORUS 3: Is it a situation of dire consequence –

CHORUS 2: A situation of urgent concern –

CHORUS 3: An inconsequential application –

CHORUS 2: Or a minor and insignificant application –

ROCHELLE: Well, let me tell you for what. My husband worked your Vessel of Opportunity programme and –

CHORUS 2: I think you'll find that everything is on the website –

CURTIS: If our questions had been –

ROCHELLE: Y'all have taken the liberty –

CHORUS 2: Please don't take that tone with me.

CHORUS 3: Well, then you'll need packets A-F.

ROCHELLE: Of making sure to bend us over – -

CHORUS 2: Did you fail the first round of –

ROCHELLE: Now, I have been to this office five times. And I have made more than 50 phone calls…and I have had absolutely no joy. ALRIGHT? My time – -is worthwhile. I have other things to do…like put my freaking life together. Alright. So I WILL see Nobodaddy or whatever the hell his name is today – ALRIGHT?

A beat.

CHORUS 3: I would suggest taking the appendix as well in that case.

She takes out a huge book from below her desk and hands it over to ROCHELLE.

CHORUS 3: If you can't find the solutions in there –

CHORUS 2: *(They are chuckling over this now.)* Then they don't exist.

ROCHELLE: And I for one would like an answer NOW –
you'd better get Ken Feinberg out here or I am gonna go
straight-up ape shit –

The CHORUS gasp at the mention of his name.

Blackout.

SCENE 3

KELLY: Feinberg – shit – I – can you delete me saying that?
(Beat.) THE Company is making us look like we're putting
out an open hand, waiting for it to fill up like a lucky slot
machine. *(Beat.)* Well, that's not the story at'tall. *(Beat.)* We
were feeding the world – *(Beat.)* It's not like we're saying
to ourselves – 'Hot damn'. We don't have to work for three
years. We can live off THE Company (yeah right.) – and
get a fat compensation pay-off. 'Well, THE Company
and – Nobodaddy – they ain't done a thing! They're just
sitting around, letting us die at high noon. I would rather
work any day, I'd rather work. I'd be fucking delighted
if the Gulf was clean, and I could go back down to ocean
front – watch the sunrise on a Saturday like I used to. But I
doubt I'll ever be able to… *(Beat.)* How do I know the oil's
still there? It's right where it was before. I go out into the
Mississippi and, come home? The propeller's covered in it.
Smell's overwhelming – makes your eyes and throat burn.
Notice all along here. This time 'a year, we usually get kids
coming down for spring break.*(Beat.)* Used to do it myself,
before me and my husband moved back. And, between
us – we stare at each other at night wonderin' how we're
ever gonna be the same. My niece Tamara – she's four this
year. My brother lets her play out on the water – running
out by the shoreline. You can see the tar balls washing up
– laying there in the sand. Somma them as big as my fists –
and he just leaves her out there, filling those stupid plastic
sandcastle buckets. She's got a cough. Keep taking her to
the hospital. And doctors just send her home. She doesn't
have a fever. So apart from cough medicine – there's
nothing much they say to do. *(Beat.)* I see 'em spraying –

Starts a low rumble, like a big cat growling at you, from far
– and starts zippin' in. Movin' in on ya. *(Beat.)* Then, you
can hear the motor overhead, cuttin' into the beach – then
the sound water hittin' the roof – the colour – like a low
orange haze. Like we're in Vietnam. And we can see all
that drizzle falling. Hard not to feel they're out to get you,
like they're tryin' to get rid of – When they're spraying
so close to home. They don't want the oil on shore. Cause
people won't come to the beaches – if they're black.

SCENE 4

*In CURTIS and ROCHELLE's apartment. CURTIS sleeps. The lines
should overlap fluidly, quickly.*

VO CHORUS 1: You lost 11/ shipmates.

VO CURTIS: *(This is utterly distressing for him, especially in the
beginning.)* I hear the engines revving, / the lights are…are
glowing. I'm hearing the alarms at a constant rate.

VO CHORUS 2: *(This should flicker and fade out, as CURTIS
speaks.)* You are not a witness and have no first-hand
knowledge / of the DISASTER –

*CURTIS lays in bed. He rattles and thrashes as he sleeps, wholely
wracked by the ghosts of the explosion.*

VO CHORUS 3: It blinded 'n wrapped round ma face. I's
thrown head-down knocked me dead-unconscious.
Moment before I blacked / …All'a could think on was –

VO CHORUS 1: You're smashed, a chicken under a grinder.
Charlie, he'd run from the comms room, / barely got out.
His head's bleedin' like you'd think he didn't have any
brain left, and he looks at me and jumps – I seen him
break as he landed, like he was made of cardboard –

*Sounds of chaos, of a fiery inferno. The consuming oil, rising in his
dreams.*

VO ROCHELLE: *(Her voice should interject, like a kind of saving
grace. A fierce bastion of sanity, for him. She peels back the*

film – .) Let me see – my husband. No I will not goddamned hold on! You got my husband locked in there twenty hours and you ain't gonna let me in to hold him. You gotta be freakin' – I mean, you gotta be kidding me –

CURTIS: Chelle! Chelle!

He wrenches into another dreaming state, this more real than the previous.

CURTIS: Ain't going back in…ain't gonna do it. Not now – -not – -

VO CHORUS 1: YOU can't leave me –

VO CHORUS 1: You was always gonna walk away.

VO CHORUS 2: Only the weakest kind of man that sees a shipmate fall and keeps running for his own life.

A beat. The CHORUS enter.

CHORUS 2: Is your life worth so much? Are you so much better than me?

CHORUS 3: Is living all that great Curtis?

CHORUS 2: I didn't have anybody. Maybe it's better I was the one – -to go…maybe it's better you left me behind… cause there's something about a full body burn tends to make people nervous.

CHORUS 2: I used to brush my baby Annabelle's hair one hundred times every night before she went to bed. With a brush my Momma gave me – that was her Momma's before. Annabelle died in her sleep, did you hear? – My baby's hair strangled clean round her neck – cause I wasn't there to take out the knots…

CURTIS: I didn't see you – I didn't see you –

CHORUS 2: Liar. I seen the rounds of your iris when the flames went up –

CURTIS: What was I supposed to do? Nothin' I coulda done.

CHORUS 3: In the end, all that talk of loyalty…no one person for themself – -it was all a lot of bullshit…

CURTIS: I'm sorry…I'm – -I'm sorry –

CHORUS 3: When a man's got his mouth round the barrel –

CURTIS: If I'd have turned back…we both would have…

CHORUS 2: Took me five hours…to die.

CURTIS: You were too far away – -all them…cans, lying round the deck. They was like…bombs, exploding. I didn't – it was like fucking Baghdad. You knew there wasn't no chance in hell I was gonna make it through. You knew I never would – that's why you didn't scream – -

CHORUS 3: I couldn't. Skin on my lips / melted clear –

CURTIS: No – no, you knew. / You knew I'd never get through – you saw that beam coming from the derrick above, you knew plain's day that beam was gonna crack – -there wasn't no way I was gonna. If I didn't have –

CHORUS 2: The lies a man will whisper to himself to ease a guilty conscience –

CHORUS 3: Well, it don't matter you didn't come last time… you come get me now cher, come on back.

CURTIS: I'm not going back – I'm not going back!

CHORUS 2: Oh baby – -but you is! You goin' back right now!

CURTIS: You get the hell away from me – -you leave me the fuck alone –

CHORUS 2: Second you start proclaiming something's never gonna get you, it starts making Christmas with your neck.

CHORUS 3: You coming with me baby…on one hell a fiery fucking bronco ride. Ask me nicely, I let you be on top.

The sound of the helicopters, passing overhead. The metallic sound of the rig crashing, breaking. The CHORUS exits – or disappears into the audience.

A beat.

CURTIS: *(Waking, from all the dream levels. He breathes heavily –
he catches his breath. He chokes. He seizes his breath – sharply.)*
Rochelle!!!

ROCHELLE enters.

ROCHELLE: What's the matter baby? –

*She kisses him and holds him as he sits, shell-shocked…Hallucinating
between this world and the second – mythic dream world which
plagues him.*

*He closes his eyes and begins to drift off… as she holds him tightly,
lovingly.*

ROCHELLE: Now listen up spirits – You think I don't know
you're here…well, I do. I got you all over my palms…and
I know what you is…I got you in my pockets. I got you
under my feet. You ain't gonna get in here no more, you
ain't gonna come in…messin' with me, cursing my love.
…Ain't no raggedy old bones set through me now – -ain't
no meat-flapping jaws gonna eat their way inside… *(Beat.)*
I didn't think so – -you looking to get somebody. Well, you
picked the wrong woman to fuck with!

Blackout.

SCENE 5

NANCY addresses her audience – a group of scientists, doctors, etc.

NANCY: Thank you for coming. I know that some of you have
journeyed here…with possible great risk to yourselves.
And – I want you to know that I appreciate your efforts.
There are times when I believe we all feel we are
screaming inside a vaccuum. That our lungs could not be
any more full with the bellows for this fight. But – I urge
you, I – implore you to keep your spirits high. To continue
to work…with me and with each other. I…offered my
research to the THE Company as many of you know.
I have now had my response. It is as we thought. They
are refusing to examine external water and sample tests.

(Beat.) Some of you may have read my findings, but for those of you who I am only reaching now…Our clean-up workers. They've all come down with one sort of nasty cancer or another. I have collected the testimonies, the information. I have made the archives for the Disaster…I have seen whales, dolphins, people…They always look half-eaten, like acid has corroded. This stuff. It attacks your fatty membranes. That's what most people don't realise. So many people – are experiencing serious pyschological and neuromotor problems. The dispersant, it gets in around your cells, and it eats them whole. And the brain – well, that's the fattiest organ in your body. So, I've…seen and am seeing people coming down with dementia-like, Alzheimer-like symptoms, MS symptoms. People ask me – if this is really happening, why are people not protesting the THE Company together? Ultimately. There is no united front. *(Beat.)* We don't all feel the same way about fossil fuels. We don't all care equally about the environment. It's not…clear cut. All we know is that everyone is suffering. And…all we want. I don't want to take anyone down…I just want someone to set up a heatlth clinic. To give people basic compensation for – income they've lost becuase they can't fish…or run their B&B… or maintain a restaurant…or be an oil worker. All people want is what is fair. No one's asking for a hand-out. That's not what this is about. It's not a major political statement, it's just…a desire to get by…

A pause.

NANCY: We have two wonderful physicians, Dr. Matt Rubineaux and Dr Wanda Sunders who have bravely offered to be here…to test all of us. If you would be willing – what they can gather from this will be invaluable for our research…and for the fight…

A quick change to the next scene.

SCENE 6

The INTERVIEWER should be brusque and unfeeling, utterly unsympathetic. She should be interviewing CURTIS as if she were addressing financial regulation, not a traumatic event from his received memory. The scene should be hyper-real, the lights should occasionally flicker. CURTIS should seem ultra-uncomfortable.

CHORUS 1: Tonight, we are here on Faux News, live with Curtis LaFontaine, survivor of THE DISASTER. I want to talk to you today about what happened to you. You were on the firefighting team – correct?

CURTIS: Yes...yes, that is correct.

CHORUS 1: So what happened, what were the events of the... night?

CURTIS: Well...I woke up to an explosion. I turned and I sat at the edge of ma bed. I'm...And the force – clear threw me across my room – into the fire-rated doors. These are three-inch thick, steel-doors...and it clear knocked me out. When I came to, smoke was already eating into the room and...I was bleeding from...what I know now was my head. And it was...thick, like pudding – just coming down into my eyes. I finally managed to get out onto the deck of the rig. Where I got slammed again by flying debris – clear knocked me to the floor below. And at this point, there are petroluem cans, and greasers, and all sorts of things which we use...everyday to keep our systems ticking. And they were all exploding, like the most intense fire-crackers you could imagine. It was like...it was like...Baghdad on the deck... When I finally managed to make my way down to the derrick – to the fire station – it was consumed by fire, it was like... I knew there was no way we were gonna put that out. I knew we should abandon the rig...

CHORUS 1: How did you feel – when you saw the derrick on fire? Did you think you...might not survive?

CURTIS: Absolutely. I was still kinda in shock. The main thing going through my head was – we're all dead. There's no way we're gettin' off here. As we were getting our gear on…we saw the crane operator get knocked forty, fifty feet from the derrick, clean to the bottom deck. *(Beat.)* We dressed out as fast as – We started trying to make our way over to get him…and flames surrounded us in every direction…and there was no way we could get him. *(A pause.)* We…I…had to leave him.

CHORUS 1: As a trained emergency professional, someone who is trained to save people, how did you feel watching that man perish?

CURTIS: *(He gulps. He clears his throat. He is nearly sweating he is so distressed by the question.)* It was…the worst…thing I've ever had to do. It haunts me today…I can't stop asking myself…is there any other way I coulda gotten over there?

A pause.

CHORUS 1: You lost colleagues as well…in the fire?

CURTIS: Yeah…yeah. I mean…you know, it burns a hole inside you, losing one of your own…But, we know it's… part of what we're trained to expect…part of – what we know could happen. Losing someone we're meant to protect. Somehow it's worse. And it ain't like – they was just members of the public. Losing someone is never easy…it always feels like you've failed – But on a rig – you're a family. Eighteen hours a day, every day…you ain't got your wife and kids around, you got – your… *(He faulters, for lack of a better word.)*…people become –

CHORUS 1: How did people manage to evacuate?

CURTIS: Well…when it came down to the day. The actual fire. Nothing went like it was supposed to. There were… problems in the engine room. The blowout preventer… That's supposed to – well stop a blowout – and to isolate the rig – and that didn't work, obviously. And then, also, none of the fire-safety mechanisms worked either. So, basically, all the things which were meant to keep us safe,

turned on us…It was just us men – fighting that fire, with…
basic equipment.

CHORUS 1: Was there panic, in terms of getting on the
lifeboats?

CURTIS: There was…in terms of…some people were – losing
it. *(Beat.)* The first two lifeboats, they left before…a
number of people could get on. So some people were
jumpin' off the rig, into the water, which was also covered
in oil, and on fire… And you got people, just scrambling
to get on. Everyone is just thinking the same thing – I got
people at home…I got people that need me…Some of
the ones left behind managed to get one of the life rafts
inflated…and it…got stuck, at a forty-five degree angle to
the side of the rig. And it was just…it was dangling, with
people falling out. And others were jumping… Thank God
they managed to get that down in the end, 'cause it looked
– it looked like they wasn't gonna make it.

*The screams of the man he left behind, echoes in the background.
It should grow increasingly louder, hollow. CURTIS should see the
MAN, he should be his focal point. His psychological state, as the
scene progresses, should break-down.*

CHORUS 1: At any point, did you consider jumping?

CURTIS: We stayed behind…after we could get most of the
men onto the other two usable life rafts. The rafts, they're
on the deck. And we had to inflate them – and get in them,
and then…get ourselves down the water. *(Beat.)* And
then, we couldn't…get the motor that inflates it…and also
propels it to start-up. So, yeah…yeah. I thought…about it.
I was fixing to –

CHORUS 1: *(Unfeelingly, with absolutely no emotion or compassion.
This should be comically cold.)* So you eventually made it to
a supply ship and back to shore, where you were asked to
sign this waiver saying you had no first hand knowledge of
how the accident occurred and that you were not injured
in the disaster. Why do you feel they asked you to sign
this?

CURTIS: Me and my wife, we were gonna leave the hotel where they put us. And…They told me it was just a statement saying I was off-tower that I wasn't working… and me and my wife, we just wanted to get out…ta go be with ma family. And…they said…it was just…to say I didn't see it all before the fire. And they just said, sign here, initial here.

CHORUS 1: What are you contending in your law suit regarding this waiver?

CURTIS: I understand they have a right to look into my claim because I signed and all, but the fact that they kept me and the other crew members off shore for 20 hours. It was…it was…you give your life to this job. People I knew and…cared about died in this incident. My lawyer, he's a maritime specialist – and people get injured all the time – -and they helicopter them in! We –

CHORUS 1: *(Interrupting. Arrogant. Sarcastic even.)* So are you saying…that it was premature for anyone to sign a waiver claiming non-injury, because, as you say, in your lawsuit that you suffer from Post Traumatic Stress Disorder?

CURTIS: I was up for 60 hours, and they are trying to use this waiver against my defence.

CHORUS 1: THE Company say, that they were surprised to receive your claim, given that you signed the waiver.

CURTIS: It just shows you that they were irresponsible and that they wanted to keep us off-shore. They could have easily brought us –

CHORUS 1: *(Interrupting.)* What health problems do you claim you have suffered?

CURTIS: *(Having difficulty expressing his stress.)* I –

CHORUS 1: Okay, well Curtis. Thank you – now back to you in the studio.

The camera stops rolling and the stage the INTERVIEWER occupies goes black. The spotlight on CURTIS. His own internal mental scape.

The sound of discordant House/Trance, mixed with faint screams. The screams get louder – until they reach a climax. And then – Blackout.

A quick, aggressive blackout.

SCENE 7

NANCY edits footage. She attempts to compile another series of interviews. She pauses and examines the painting. The sound of heavy footsteps in the background. A creaking door. The bathroom opens. Blackout.

SCENE 8

CURTIS on his porch, as before. This time. He is lighter – he has entered a different kind of psychic state. He is clearer.

CURTIS: *(Sung.)* Lennard's song 2.

ROCHELLE enters at the end of the scene, slowly. CURTIS does not hear her. As he finishes playing, she comes to him from behind and kisses him. She kneels next to him and they hold each other tightly.

The sound of a ticking geiger counter.

Blackout.

SCENE 9

NANCY is outside collecting samples of the oiled sand and water. ROCHELLE, hearing her, exits outside to see what she is doing.

ROCHELLE: *(Entering.)* What are you doing?

CURTIS: *(Entering.)* Dinner's ready baby – Jesus Christ! Do you know what time it is – Are you trying to – I'm going inside and I swear to God you'd both better not be far behind me.

CURTIS exits.

ROCHELLE: Do you know how much –

NANCY: Shhh! Come, / help me.

ROCHELLE: I could hear you all the way / to the house!

NANCY: You could not. You were watching. The light was on.

ROCHELLE: They're going to find you.

NANCY: I don't care – if they find me or not.

ROCHELLE: You should care. You're gonna get yourself –

NANCY: Way I see it, I'm already in a fucklot of trouble, and I haven't done anything wrong. So I may as well earn it.

ROCHELLE: This is insane!

NANCY: You should just go – I'll tell them you didn't know a thing.

ROCHELLE: I know you've been out here digging and taking samples for hours.

NANCY: Wrong – I'm making sandcastles. They're better by night. *(Pause.)* You should go. You should stay away in fact.

A beat.

NANCY: They'll be coming soon.

A beat.

NANCY: I won't name you, don't worry –

ROCHELLE: They'll take you.

NANCY: Of course they will.

ROCHELLE: You aren't afraid?

NANCY: Aren't we all afraid now.

ROCHELLE: You should give me the research so they don't –

NANCY hands ROCHELLE a key – and then she continues digging, pulling out skeletons...

NANCY: They'll be here any moment. You need to leave.

The sounds of a raging machine, a tank growing closer. The slushing of oil. A pause. Blackout. A gunshot.

SCENE 10

EMCEE: Please welcome back – The Oracles for their last song of the night – -

The CHORUS drink a great long swig of alcohol. CHORUS 3 raises it to the audience and then pours a little on the ground.

CHORUS 1: How high's the water?

The CHORUS look around, carefully and lower their voices.

CHORUS 1: Never said it was a happy story…

CHORUS 2: Never even promised you'd like it…

CHORUS 3: But it's in your blood –

CHORUS 3: You're a story-teller now.

CHORUS 2: *(Singing.)* This little light of mine –

CHORUS 1: I'm gonna let it shine.

EMCEE: This little light of mine –

CHORUS 3: I'm gonna let it shine.

ALL: Let it shine – let it shine – let it shine.

CHORUS 1: I'm gonna –

CHORUS 2: Let it –

EMCEE: Shine – shine – shine –

CHORUS 3: *(Overlapping with CHORUS all.)* This little light of mine! I'm gonna let it shine. Ohh, I'm gonna let it shine. Ohh, I'm gonna let it shine. Oohh, I'm gonna let it shine.

Blackout.

Curtain.